# Picture Punch

### cards for all seasons

**Marianne Zimny**

FORTE PUBLISHERS

# Contents

ISBN 90 5877 457 0

This is a publication from
Forte Publishers BV
P.O. Box 1394
3500 BJ Utrecht
The Netherlands

For more information about the creative books available from
Forte Uitgevers:
www.forteuitgevers.nl

Final editing: Gina Kors-Lambers, Steenwijk, the Netherlands
Photography and digital image editing: Fotografie Gerhard Witteveen, Apeldoorn, the Netherlands
Cover and inner design:
BADE creatieve communicatie, Baarn, the Netherlands
Translation: Michael Ford, TextCase, Hilversum, the Netherlands

| | |
|---|---|
| Preface | 3 |
| Techniques | 4 |
| Step-by-step | 5 |
| Materials | 6 |
| Spring flowers | 7 |
| Lovers | 10 |
| Birth | 14 |
| Party | 16 |
| Holiday | 18 |
| Get well soon | 22 |
| Autumn weather | 24 |
| Christmas feeling | 27 |
| Christmas party | 30 |

# Preface

When I drew my first Picture Punch sheet more than two years ago,
I could not have imagined they would be such a huge success. Now, more
than 100 Picture Punch sheets later, it seemed a good idea to write this
book and to show you that you can do much more with the sheets.

Picture Punch cards for all seasons will show you that you can make
Picture Punch cards all year round. The charming spring cards,
happy summer cards, robust autumn cards and ice-cold winter
cards have all been made using Picture Punch sheets. By cutting
the frames and the borders in different ways, by using different
types of paper and different colours, and by using the new
paper fasteners, I hope I have shown you that there are many
different possibilities.

*Marianne*

I really enjoyed writing this book and I hope you will enjoy making the cards just as much.

# Techniques

Picture Punch is an easy 3D technique where the figures are punched out and then stuck on the card using 3D glue. Each sheet also contains attractive borders and frames which are easy to cut out. The 3D figures all match the existing punches. On each sheet, it clearly states which punches must be used.

The figures on the Picture Punch sheets have all been drawn as a mirror image, so that you can easily punch them out holding the punch upside down and so that you can see exactly what you are doing. Make sure to always cut a strip of several figures, because that makes it easier to punch.

Lay out everything you need before you start. First, cut the squares, borders and frames out of the Picture Punch sheet. Next, cut the sheet into strips. Turn the punch upside down and carefully punch out the figures. Cut and glue the card as described in the instructions and finally use 3D glue to stick the punched figures on the card. Tweezers with a pointed end are very useful for that, in particular for the small figures. It is recommended to use a glue syringe to apply the 3D glue, because that makes it easier to apply the glue, also on the smaller parts.

## Using a frame ruler

The frame rulers are a vital tool for making almost all the cards in this book. You can use a frame ruler for all the cutting work. It makes it very easy to cut the frames and squares. There are detailed instructions with every frame ruler. Read these carefully before using the frame ruler. It is very easy to cut a square or an A6 card using a frame ruler. To make a square card, fold an A4 card double widthways. To make a nice fold line, use the ruler to first score the card with an embossing stylus.

Place the square frame ruler against the fold on the double folded card and cut off the excess paper around the ruler to give you a perfect square card. To make an A6 card, cut an A4 card in two widthways. Use the frame ruler and an embossing stylus to make a score line exactly in the middle.

## Using the Orbis circle cutter

This circle cutter easily cuts round frames and very narrow circle borders. To cut a round frame, place the card on your cutting mat and, if necessary, stick it down using pieces of crêpe adhesive tape to stop it sliding about. If necessary, make a small pencil mark to indicate the middle. Place the cutting point of the lines

1. The materials for Picture Punch.

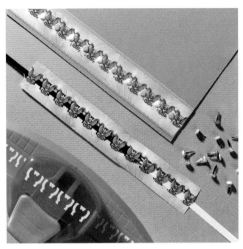

2. Punch the strip, thread a strip of weaving paper through it and decorate it with paper fasteners.

3. Cut strips and punch separate figures.

4. Use 3D glue to stick the figures on the card.

on the circle cutter on the pencil mark and place the point of the knife perpendicular in the desired hole. Make sure the cutting side of the knife is pointing in the cutting direction. Firmly push the green border of the circle cutter with your free hand onto the paper and slowly turn it. Do not try to cut the paper in one go. It is better to cut it using two or three turns of the circle cutter. This will make the knife last longer and will also prevent the paper from moving or the knife from getting stuck in the cutting mat. When cutting borders, start by cutting the inner circle. Next, move the knife to the outside without moving the circle cutter itself.

## Adding paper fasteners

Paper fasteners are not only used to decorate the cards, but can also be used as a rotating point or for attaching punched figures.
It is easiest to add them if you first prick a hole where you wish to have the paper fastener. To do this, use a perforating tool and a pricking mat.

# Materials

- ❏ Card
- ❏ Picture Punch sheets
- ❏ Allura transparent vellum and embossing vellum
- ❏ Paper fasteners
- ❏ Frame rulers: 14 x 14 cm and A6
- ❏ Various punches

- ❏ Embossing templates
- ❏ 3D glue and a syringe
- ❏ Cutting mat and knife
- ❏ Tweezer scissors
- ❏ Scissors
- ❏ Double-sided adhesive tape
- ❏ Photo glue

- ❏ Perforating tool and a pricking mat
- ❏ Embossing stylus
- ❏ Weaving needle
- ❏ Vellum spray
- ❏ Orbis circle cutter

# Spring flowers

The best thing about summer is the blossoming flowers. These charming flower cards will put you in the right mood straight away.

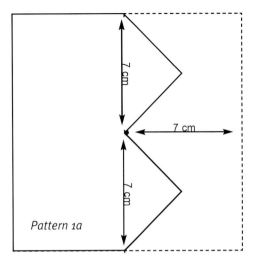

Pattern 1a

**What you need:**
- ❏ Aqua marine square card
- ❏ Florence paper: green and yellow
- ❏ Paper strips for weaving: blue and yellow
- ❏ Picture Punch sheet: lily
- ❏ Allura embossing vellum: lily
- ❏ Embossing stencil: lily
- ❏ Mosaic punch
- ❏ Daisy punch
- ❏ Paper fasteners: pale yellow, pink and light blue
- ❏ Border punch: weave star

## 1. Square card with a mosaic border
Make a double card (8 x 14 cm) from yellow paper. Cut 8 cm from the front of a blue card to leave a 6 cm wide strip. Stick the yellow card the other way around on the blue card to make a triptych. Use the mosaic punch to punch a mosaic border on the blue strip starting from the middle. Make sure the edges of the punch openings just touch each other to create an attractive open border. Use the mosaic punch to punch three yellow and two green figures and cut the corners loose. Punch daisies from the Picture Punch sheet and use yellow paper fasteners to attach them, together with the green and yellow mosaic figures, on the card's mosaic border. Cut a strip (3 x 14 cm) and a square (5.5 x 5.5 cm) out of blue card. Cut the green flower border out of the Picture Punch sheet and stick it on the blue strip. Punch four daisies and use yellow paper fasteners to attach them to the strip (only the two outer

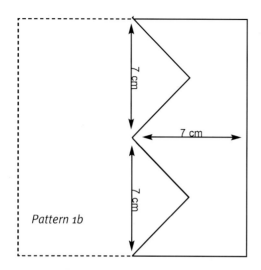

Pattern 1b

7 cm

7 cm

7 cm

7 cm

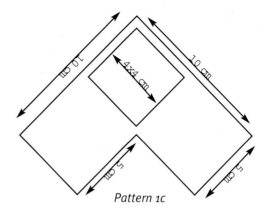

10 cm

10 cm

4 x 4 cm

5 cm

5 cm

Pattern 1c

daisies on both sides). Stick the strip on the yellow side of the card. Stick the blue square diagonally in the middle of this strip. Cut and punch a square from the Picture Punch sheet and punch the separate mosaic figure and two daisies. Use a yellow paper fastener to attach them to the Picture Punch square and stick this on the blue square. Cut the lily strip out of the Picture Punch sheet and punch the border. Weave a yellow strip of weaving paper through it. Prick holes between the flowers and alternately push pink and blue paper fasteners into the holes. Open the rear of the paper fasteners and push them flat. Stick the strip in the card on the transition between the green and the yellow.

## 2. A6 card with an embossed lily

Cut the frame with the lilies out of the embossing paper and emboss it. Use an A6 frame ruler to cut a frame (8 x 6 cm) out of the front of a blue A6 card. Cut the lily frame out of the Picture Punch sheet and cut out the inside. Use the border punch to punch the border and weave yellow strips of weaving paper through it. Prick holes between the flowers on the yellow strip and push blue and pink paper fasteners into the holes. Open the rear of the paper fasteners and push them flat. Stick the embossing paper behind the Picture Punch frame and stick it on the card exactly in front of the cut out frame. Stick a piece of green paper (7 x 9 cm) in the card and stick the yellow card with the lily from the Picture Punch sheet on it.

## 3. Square card with four squares

Use the frame ruler to make a square card from green paper. Cut this card according to pattern

1.

2.

3.

1a. Cut the blue card according to pattern 1b. Stick both cards together and stick a yellow square (14 x 14) inside. Cut pattern 1c out of yellow paper. Stick the separate parts together. Cut and punch the squares out of the Picture Punch sheet. Punch green and coloured daisies and use yellow paper fasteners to attach them to the punched squares (prick holes in each part first to make it easier). Stick the squares on the card. Cut a rectangle (7 x 14 cm) out of the transparent paper and use vellum spray to stick this on the right-hand side of the card under the green side. Make a green square (4.5 x 4.5 cm) and stick this behind the opening in the card. Add a suitable text sticker.

# Lovers

*A springtime feeling or butterflies in your stomach. They feel almost the same. You get that same feeling from these lovers cards.*

*What you need:*
❏ *Card: two light blue square cards, two pink square cards, one light blue A6 card and one pink A6 card*
❏ *Paper fasteners: medium white heart and white circle*
❏ *Picture Punch sheet*

❏ *Double silhouette punch: bell*
❏ *Silhouette punch: lovers*
❏ *Punch with push button: heart*
❏ *Mini distance punch: heart*

## 1. A6 card with circles

Use the pink and the blue A6 cards. Cut the cards according to pattern 2 and stick the pink card in the blue card so that the wavy lines are aligned. Cut out two circle borders: a pink border with an inside diameter of 6 cm and an outside diameter of 7 cm and a blue border with an inside diameter of 5 cm and an outside diameter of 6 cm. Stick the blue border on the pink flap of the card and the pink border on the blue flap around the middle semicircle. Use the perforating tool to prick five holes in the pink flap and five holes in the blue flap 0.5 cm from the outside edge of the circle borders. Put white paper fasteners (hearts) in the holes. Cut three circles with pictures out of the Picture Punch sheet: two blue circles with heads and a pink circle with a bell. Punch the middle and use 3D glue to stick the pictures on the card. Punch two separate heads and a bell and cut loose the collar and the corners. Use 3D glue to stick them on the pictures.

## 2. Square card with borders

Cut an incision in the front of the card 4 cm from the top and bottom edges to the fold so that the front flap of the card is divided into three. Cut off the two outer flaps of the blue card along the fold and the middle flap of the pink card. Stick the pink card in the blue card with the fold on the right-hand side. Cut the borders out of the Picture Punch sheet. Punch the wide border and use 3D glue to stick this on the blue middle part of the card. Cut two blue strips (2.5 x14 cm) and stick the heart borders from the Picture Punch sheet on them, paying attention to the direction in which the hearts face. Next, prick a hole above and/or below each heart 0.5 cm from the border. Put round white paper fasteners in the holes and push the back of the fasteners flat.
Stick the borders on the card 0.5 cm from the top and bottom. Punch some loose figures, cut them loose and stick them on the card in 3D.

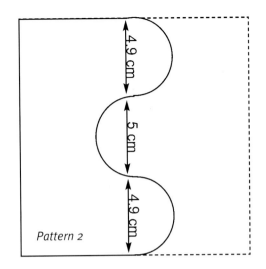

Pattern 2

4.9 cm

5 cm

4.9 cm

## 3. Square card with a circle

Cut a circle (Ø 55 mm) exactly in the middle of the front of a square pink card. Use a circle cutter to round off the outer corners of the front of the card. Cut the large circle out of the Picture Punch sheet. Cut out the inner circle, punch the silhouettes and stick the circle on the front of the card. Cut a blue card along the fold and attach two white paper fasteners in two corners. Prick the holes 1 cm from the sides. Close the card and stick the middle circle with bells exactly in the middle of the round frame in the card. Punch heads and bells out of the Picture Punch sheet and cut the collars and the corners loose. Use 3D glue to stick the shapes on the card. Punch some hearts and stick some of them in 3D on the card.

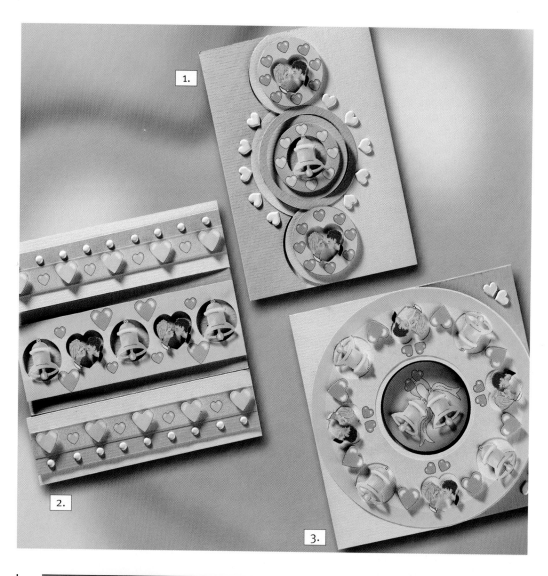

1.

2.

3.

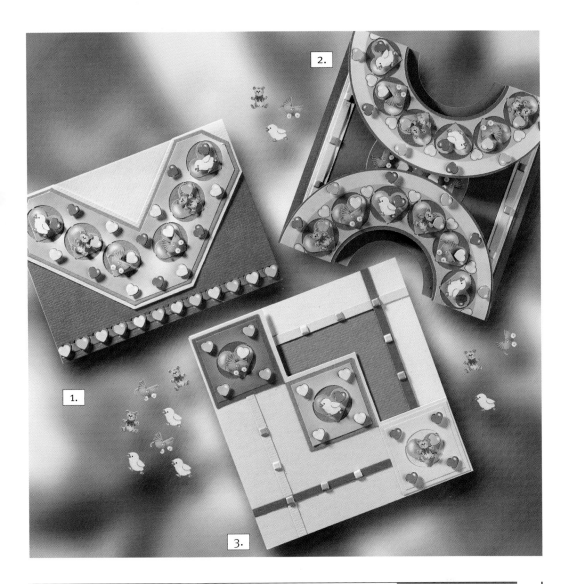

# Birth

Spring and a new birth belong together. Look at nature and you will know exactly what I mean.

*What you need:*
- ❏ *Florence paper: red, yellow, cream and aqua marine*
- ❏ *Picture Punch sheet: baby*
- ❏ *Paper fasteners: square mini pastel*
- ❏ *Punches: pram, bear, chick and mini heart*
- ❏ *Weave border punch: heart*
- ❏ *Paper strips for weaving: blue, yellow and red*

## 1. Rectangular card with a braided border

Cut the front of the yellow card according to pattern 3. Cut the Picture Punch border out and cut the corners off at an angle 1 cm from the corner. Punch the border, stick it on the blue card and cut the blue card along the Picture Punch border leaving a 2 mm wide blue border. Stick this on the front of the card. Cut a rectangle (10.5 x 14.8 cm) out of red card and use the border punch to punch a border in a long side. Weave a blue strip of weaving paper through it and stick the rectangle in the card with the embroidered border on the outside of the card. Punch figures and use 3D glue to stick them on the card. Punch yellow and blue hearts and stick them on the embroidered border.

## 2. Square triptych card with semicircles

Cut a rectangle (14 x 28 cm). Score the card twice widthways 7 cm from the edge. Use a

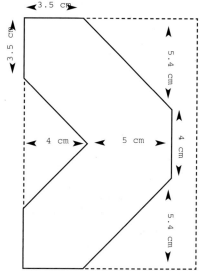

*Pattern 3*

pencil to mark the middle of the score lines and cut out two circles (Ø 6.5 cm) with these points as the centre. Use a circle cutter to round off the left-hand and the right-hand side of the card. Fold the triptych. Cut a square (14 x 14 cm) out of the aqua marine card. Cut a semicircle (Ø 5 cm) in both sides. Cut two strips (14 x 1 cm) from cream card and stick yellow strips of weaving paper on them. Prick five holes in the middle of the yellow strip and put pastel paper fasteners in them. Stick these borders above and below the blue square and then stick this in the card. Cut the large circle out of the Picture Punch sheet, cut out the middle circle and punch the border starting from the middle. Cut the border in two and stick them on the front of the card. Stick the middle circle in the middle of the blue part of the card. Punch bears, prams, chicks and hearts and use 3D glue to stick them on the card.

### 3. Square baby card with three squares

Use the frame ruler to cut the card according to pattern 4, starting at the top 5 cm from the fold. Cut 4.5 cm downwards, then 4.5 cm to the right, 4.5 cm downwards again and then another 4.5 cm to the right. Stick a cream square (14 x 14 cm) in the card. Cut a blue square (10 x

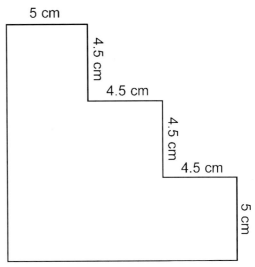

*Pattern 4*

10 cm) and stick it in the card. Stick red and yellow strips of weaving paper over the top and right-hand side of the blue square and have these strips continue to the edge of the card. Attach paper fasteners to them. Stick strips of weaving paper on the front of the card 2 cm from the edge and attach paper fasteners to them. Cut squares (4.5 x 4.5 cm) out of red, blue and yellow card and stick these on the card 2.5 mm from the edge. Cut the squares out of the Picture Punch sheet, punch them and stick them on the card. Punch the separate figures and use 3D glue to stick them on the card.

# Party

*Cheerful clowns for a great garden party on your birthday on a lovely summer's day.*

*What you need:*
- ❏ *Structure card: aqua marine, red and yellow*
- ❏ *Florence card: bright green*
- ❏ *Picture Punch sheet: birthday/clown*
- ❏ *Punches: balloon, clown and sweet*
- ❏ *Balloon paper fasteners:*
  *blue, yellow and red*
- ❏ *Mini square paper fasteners:*
  *orange, yellow and green*

## 1. Square red card with a circle

Use the frame ruler to make a square card from red structure card (see Techniques). Cut the circle out of the Picture Punch sheet. Start with the smallest circle and cut all the borders loose from the inside to the outside. If you find it difficult using the circle cutter, then you can also cut the borders with scissors. Use the tweezer scissors to prick a small hole in the white border between the circles and then carefully cut them out. Cut a circle (Ø 82 mm) out of the front of the card using the Orbis circle cutter.

This cutter allows you to accurately set the diameter. Cut a circle border out of yellow card with an outside diameter of 14 cm and an inside diameter of 7.8 cm. Stick this circle behind the front of the card. Stick the circle border with sweets on the card as well as the circle border with balloons. Cut a circle (Ø 90 mm) out of green Florence card and stick the circle with the clowns and the sweets on it. Use a balloon paper fastener to attach this circle to the middle of the card. Punch balloons, sweets and clowns out of the Picture Punch sheet and use 3D glue to stick them on the card.

## 2. A6 card with balloon lock

Use the frame ruler to make an A6 double card from blue card (see Techniques). Cut 2.5 cm off the front. Cut a strip (4 x 14.8 cm) from red card and prick five holes in it 1.2 cm from the edge, starting with the middle hole. Put paper fasteners in the four outer holes and stick the strip in the card. Prick the middle hole. This will be used to keep the card closed. Cut a strip (21 x 2.5 cm) from green Florence card and fold it double. Stick it exactly in the middle of the card.

## 3. Square card with borders

Cut a rectangle (23 x 14 cm) out of yellow card

1.

2.

3.

and score a line on both sides 4.5 cm from the edge. Fold the card to make a triptych. Cut two strips (5.5 x 14 cm) out of blue card and stick these behind the two flaps of the card so that a 1 cm wide border protrudes. Divide five paper fasteners evenly over the blue borders. Cut a rectangle (5 x 14 cm) out of red card and stick it exactly in the middle of the card. Also cut a rectangle (4.5 x 14 cm) out of blue card. Cut the borders with sweets and the wide border with clowns and balloons out of the Picture Punch sheet. Stick the clown border on the blue rectangle and then use 3D glue to stick this on the red rectangle in the card. Stick the borders with sweets on the front of the card so that there is a 3 mm wide yellow border. Punch balloons, clowns and sweets and use 3D glue to stick them on the card.

# Holiday

*My favourite holiday memories are of me with my children on the beach looking for shells and crabs.*

*What you need:*
- ❏ *Cream card: two square cards and one A6 card*
- ❏ *Florence paper: ochre and aqua marine*
- ❏ *Picture Punch sheet: sea shells*
- ❏ *Allura embossing vellum*
- ❏ *Weave border punch: butterfly*
- ❏ *Punches: fish and crab*
- ❏ *Paper strips for weaving: blue and yellow*
- ❏ *Paper fasteners: white*

## 1. Square card with a fish square
Cut a square (9 x 9 cm) with a shell pattern out of Allura embossing vellum and stick it in the top left-hand corner of the card. Cut two

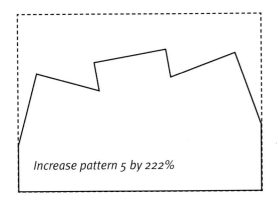

*Increase pattern 5 by 222%*

rectangles (9 x 3.5 cm) out of ochre and blue card and stick the blue rectangle under the shell square and the ochre rectangle next to the shell square. Take the blue and ochre weave borders with seahorses from the Picture Punch sheet and weave strips of blue paper through them using a weaving needle. Add white paper fasteners between the seahorses and stick the weave strips on the card. Stick the blue strip along the ochre part of the card and the ochre strip along the blue part of the card. Cut a square (5.5 x 5.5 cm) out of cream card and stick the Picture Punch square with fish on it using 3D glue. Also use 3D glue to stick the square on the card where the weave borders cross. Punch fish and use 3D glue to stick them on the fish square.

## 2. A6 card with criss-cross squares

Cut three squares (4.5 x 4.5 cm) out of ochre card and stick them on the card criss-crossing each

other. Cut the card off along the edge of the squares using pattern 5. Stick a rectangle (10.5 x 14.8 cm) in the card. Cut a strip (2.5 x 14.8 cm) out of ochre card and stick it in the card 3 mm from the edge. Cut three squares with fish out of the Picture Punch sheet and cut the ochre border off them. Also cut 14.8 cm of blue weave border with seahorses, weave a cream strip through it and add white and blue paper fasteners. Stick it on the ochre strip in the card. Use 3D glue to stick the three squares on the card. Punch separate fish and crabs and use 3D glue to stick them on the squares.

## 3. Square card with a frame

Cut a rectangle (14 x 8 cm) out of blue card and stick it on a square cream card. Use a frame ruler to cut a frame (8 x 6 cm) out of the front of the card. Cut the ochre border with fish and crabs out of the Picture Punch sheet. Cut two 14 cm long strips off of it. Stick these above and below the blue frame on the card. Stick two cream strips of weaving paper along the edge of the blue part of the card and evenly space out white and blue paper fasteners along it. Cut the seahorses and shells out and use 3D glue to stick them on the card. Punch fish and crabs and make them 3D on the card.

1.

2.

3.

# Get well soon

*A rich harvest follows a lovely summer. All the juicy autumn fruit is so wonderful.*

*What you need:*
- ❏ *Cream card:*
  *two square cards and one A6 card*
- ❏ *Florence card: pale green*
- ❏ *Linen pressing paper: orange*
- ❏ *Paper strips for weaving: orange and yellow*
- ❏ *Picture Punch sheet: fruit*
- ❏ *Weave border punch: heart*
- ❏ *Punches: leaf, apple and pear*

## 1. Square card with a fruit wreath

Make a square green card and cut a 9 cm strip off the front to leave a 5 cm wide flap. Cut 5 cm off a cream card. Stick the cream card the wrong way round in the green card so that the fronts are joined up. Use the frame ruler to cut a frame (6 x 8 cm) in the cream flap. Cut a rectangle (7 x 9 cm) out of orange card and stick it behind the frame in the card. Stick the rectangle with the fruit wreath from the Picture Punch sheet on this. Cut the weave border with apples out of the Picture Punch sheet and punch it. Cut two

9 cm long pieces off and weave an orange strip of weaving paper through it. Stick the borders on the card above and below the frame. Cut a strip (14.8 x 3.5 cm) out of orange card and stick it on the card's green flap. Cut the red fruit border out of the Picture Punch sheet and cut 14.8 cm off of it. Stick this on the orange strip and punch fruit and leaves out of the Picture Punch sheet. Use 3D glue to stick the fruit and leaves on the card. Cut the separate parts of the fruit wreath out and make them 3D on the card. It is not necessary to use all the leaves.

## 2. A6 card with a zigzag triptych

Make an A6 card out of green and cream card according to the general instructions of the frame ruler. Cut the green and the cream card according to pattern 6. Cut a frame (4 x 4 cm) in the green card 0.5 cm from the sides. Stick the cards in each other the wrong way round and stick an orange rectangle (10.5 x 14.8 cm) in the card. Stick strips of weaving paper around the edge of the card. Cut the squares with green and yellow frames out of the Picture Punch sheet and stick the square with the yellow frame in the card behind the green frame. Stick the square with the green frame on the cream side of the card. Punch separate leaves, apples and pears out of the Picture Punch sheet and stick them on the squares. Stick three pears along the cream strip of weaving paper on the card's green flap and three apples along the orange strip of weaving paper on the card's cream flap.

### 3. Square card with a diagonal frame

Make a square card out of green Florence card according to the general instructions of the frame ruler. Next, use the frame ruler to cut a frame (6 x 6 cm) in the front of the green card and in the front of a cream card. Cut the front of both cards diagonally from the top right-hand corner to the bottom left-hand corner. Stick the green card the wrong way round in the cream card. Cut the frame out of the Picture Punch sheet, cut out the middle square and cut the frame diagonally in two. Use the border punch to punch the borders, weave orange strips of weaving paper through them and stick the two halves on the card along the frame. Cut the excess paper away. Cut a square (6 x 6 cm) out of orange card and stick it in the card. Cut the square with the red border out of the Picture Punch sheet and stick it in the middle of the orange square in the card. Punch leaves, apples and a pear and use 3D glue to stick them on the card.

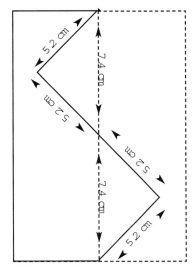

*Pattern 6*

# Autumn weather

*Autumn weather is not so nice, but the autumn colours are lovely.*

*What you need:*
- ❑ *Terracotta card: two square cards*
- ❑ *A4 terracotta card*
- ❑ *Linen pressing paper: orange*
- ❑ *Florence card: green*
- ❑ *Picture Punch sheet: autumn leaves*
- ❑ *Allura embossing vellum: autumn leaves*
- ❑ *Punches: leaf, birch leaf and maple leaf*
- ❑ *Embossing stencil: leaves*

## 1. Square card with four frames

Cut the square frame out of the Picture Punch sheet and only use the middle square without the border with acorns. Cut out three squares, leaving the orange square with the maple leaf. Place this frame diagonally on the front of a terracotta card. Cut off the right-hand corners of the terracotta card along the frame. Do not stick the frame on the card yet. Cut the three open frames out of the front of the card. Also cut the bottom frame out of the back of the card. Cut the squares with acorns and orange leaf out of the Allura embossing vellum leaving a border. Stick the acorns behind the window of the Picture Punch sheet and stick it on the card. Cut a square (14 x 14 cm) out of orange paper and cut the bottom frame out of this. Stick the transparent square with an orange leaf behind the window in the orange card and stick this on the card. Emboss the orange leaf and the acorns. Emboss the maple leaf from the transparent Allura vellum, cut it out carefully and use 3D glue to stick it on the orange frame on the card. Also emboss the brown square with the oak leaf and stick this in the card behind the right-hand frame. Also stick the ochre square with acorns behind the window in the card. Punch separate leaves and use 3D glue to stick them on the card.

## 2. Square card with an acorn border

Cut the square frame with four squares out of the Picture Punch sheet and cut the acorn border loose. Also cut out the rectangular frame from the Picture Punch sheet and cut the outer border loose. Cut a square (8.5 x 8.5 cm) out of green card and cut it diagonally to make a triangle. Stick this triangle in the top right-hand corner of the card. Stick the orange, rectangular frame with acorns

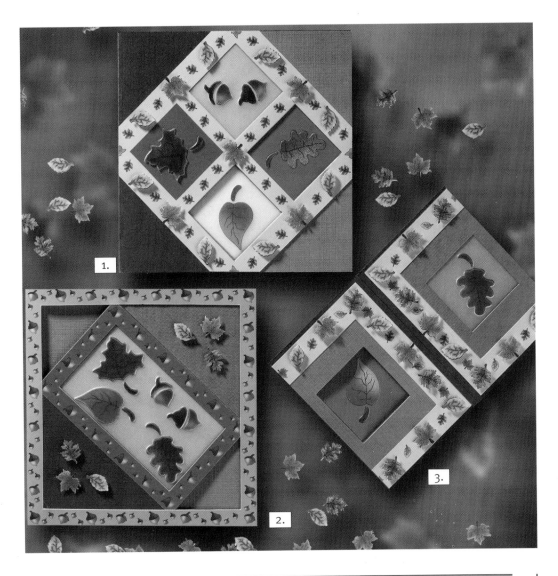

1.

2.

3.

diagonally on the front of the card and cut out the inside of the frame. Stick the square acorn border on the card. Cut away the two small triangles in the top left and bottom right-hand corners. Cut the rectangular frame, including the border, out of the Allura embossing vellum and use the embossing stylus and stencil to emboss it. Use double-sided adhesive tape to stick it behind the card's frame. Stick the rectangle from the Picture Punch sheet exactly behind the opening in the card. Punch separate leaves and use 3D glue to stick them on the terracotta and green triangles on the front of the card.

### 3. A6 triptych card
Cut an A4 terracotta card lengthways through the middle. Score two lines 7.4 cm from the shorts sides and fold the card into a triptych.

Cut the rectangular frame out of the Picture Punch sheet and cut the two borders loose. Use the border with leaves and cut it exactly through the middle.
Stick one half on an orange rectangle (7 x 10 cm) and the other half on a green rectangle of the same size. Cut a square (4 x 4 cm) out of both halves exactly in the middle of the coloured part. Place both rectangles on the front of the card with the open side of the borders facing towards the fold. Cut the inside of the frame out of the card. Use a light box when embossing the Picture Punch sheet. This is not necessary when using transparent embossing paper. Cut the square with the oak leaf out of the Allura embossing vellum leaving a border, emboss it and stick it behind the green frame. Stick both rectangles on the card. Cut two rectangles (1.5 x 5 cm) out of green and orange paper. Stick the orange rectangle behind the green frame in the card and the green rectangle behind the orange frame. Emboss the green square with the orange leaf from the Picture Punch sheet and stick it on the green rectangle exactly behind the orange window. Punch separate leaves and use 3D glue to stick them on the borders of the card.

# Christmas feeling

The Christmas feeling is great.
All the lights in the Christmas
tree are wonderful.

*What you need:*
- ❏ *Cream card: two square cards*
- ❏ *Florence card: cream, green, red and ochre*
- ❏ *Stickles glitter glue: gold*
- ❏ *Picture Punch sheet: Christmas tree*
- ❏ *Punches: Christmas wreath, Christmas stocking, stick of rock, lantern and star*

## 1. Square card with squares

Cut a square (11 x 11 cm) out of ochre card and stick it diagonally on the front of a cream square card. Cut the protruding corners off. Cut the nine small squares out of the Picture Punch sheet and stick them on red card starting with a blue square in the middle. Next, stick a beige square at every corner so that the points of the squares just touch each other. Next, stick four blue squares at the points of the beige squares to create a chessboard of squares. Cut the red card leaving a 2 mm wide border. Cut the red squares out, also leaving a 2 mm wide border. Stick the red card on the ochre card. Also cut the windows out of the ochre card. Cut a square (6 x 6 cm) out of green card, cut it diagonally in two and stick these triangles in the card in the two outer corners. Cut two 6 mm wide strips out of ochre paper and stick them 0.5 cm from the card's green corners. Cut a square (8 x 8 cm) out of red card and stick it in the middle of the card. Draw around the edges of the ochre card on the front of the card using gold glitter glue. Also add a glitter glue border along the edges of the red frames. Punch separate figures and use 3D glue to stick them on the card. Punch four stars and stick them in the frames.

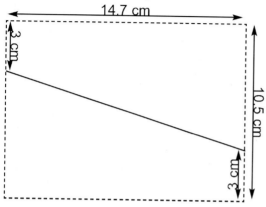

14.7 cm

3 cm

10.5 cm

3 cm

*Pattern 7*

## 2. A6 triptych with Christmas borders

Cut an A4 ochre and a cream card lengthways
through the middle. Score a line on both cards
exactly in the middle and fold the cards double
to make two A6 landscape cards. Cut both cards
according to pattern 7. Stick the ochre card the
wrong way round in the cream card. Cut a
rectangle (10.5 x 14.8 cm) out of red and green
card and cut them according to pattern 7.
Stick the red card behind the ochre flap and the
green card behind the cream flap in the card.
Cut the beige and blue borders out of the
Picture Punch sheet and stick the beige border
on green card and the blue border on red card.
Cut them out leaving a 1 mm wide border. Stick
the beige border on the ochre flap and the blue
border on the cream flap. Add a gold glitter
glue border around both borders. Punch loose
figures and cut them out. Punch six stars and
stick them along the diagonal borders.

## 3. Square card with an oval frame

Cut the oval out of the Picture Punch sheet and
cut the outer border loose. Stick this on the
front of a cream square card. Cut out the inside
of this oval (leaving a 2 mm wide border) and
cut the card off along the right-hand outside
border, also leaving a 2 mm wide border. Cut
a square (14 x 14 cm) out of ochre and green
card and cut them diagonally through the middle.
Stick an ochre and a green triangle in the card.
Stick the middle oval with a Christmas tree on
red card and cut it out leaving a 2 mm wide
border. Prick a hole in the middle of the star
and use a gold star paper fastener to attach
the oval in the card exactly behind the oval
frame. Add a glitter glue border around the
inside and outside borders of the oval frame
and also along the border of the Christmas tree
frame. Leave the glue to dry. Punch separate
figures and use 3D glue to stick them in the card.

1.

2.

3.

# Christmas party

Who says Father Christmas doesn't exist? These cards really make you doubt whether he is make-believe.

*What you need:*
- ❏ *Card: two red square cards, one yellow square card, one A6 red card and one A6 blue card*
- ❏ *Picture punch sheet: Father Christmas*
- ❏ *Allura embossing vellum: Father Christmas*
- ❏ *Stickels glitter glue: red, yellow, blue, copper and iridescent*
- ❏ *Sticker sheet with a Christmas wish*
- ❏ *Embossing stencils: Father Christmas and Christmas accessories*
- ❏ *Punches: Father Christmas, Father Christmas hat, Christmas stocking and star*
- ❏ *Paper fasteners: medium white star*

## 1. Triptych

Cut the red and the blue A6 cards according to pattern 8. Stick the red card the wrong way round in the blue card. Cut loose the yellow border of the rectangular frame of the Picture Punch sheet and cut it widthways in two. Stick both halves on the card with the borders facing towards each other and cut the protruding bits off. Cut the squares out of the square frame of the Picture Punch sheet and stick the light blue square with the Christmas stocking on a red square (4 x 4 cm) and the square with the Father Christmas hat on a blue square. Use 3D glue to raise the squares slightly. Prick two holes in the corners of both

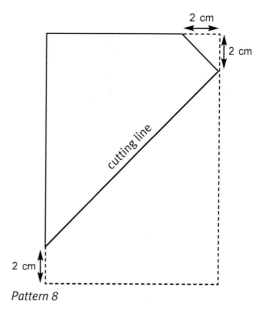

Pattern 8

frames and put two star paper fasteners in them. Draw around the edges of the Father Christmas hat and the Christmas stocking with glitter glue of a suitable colour. Punch out Father Christmases and stick them on the card in 3D.

## 2. Square card with four frames

Use the inner part of the square frame from the Picture Punch sheet without the blue border. Cut the four squares out and stick them on the front of a square red card. Cut the windows open leaving a 2 mm wide. Also cut the windows in the top right and bottom left-hand corners open in the back of the card. Cut a square (11 x 11 cm) out of cream card and also cut the two frames in it diagonally opposite each other. Stick the square frame from the Allura embossing vellum behind it and emboss the Father Christmas hat and the Christmas stocking. Stick everything in the card. Stick the squares with mittens in the card. Use blue and red glitter glue to draw around the edges of the cards. Leave the glue to dry. Punch separate figures and use 3D glue to stick them on the card.

## 3. Square triptych card

Cut a red and a yellow square card diagonally in two from the top right-hand corner to the bottom left-hand corner. Stick the red card the wrong way round in the yellow card. Cut a frame (5 x 8 cm) in the yellow card 0.5 cm from the top left-hand corner, but cut the bottom right-hand corner at an angle (1 cm from the point). Cut the square frame out of the Picture Punch sheet and cut loose the blue border with stars. Cut this diagonally through the middle and stick both halves on the front of the card. Cut the inner square with the Father Christmas out of rectangular frame of the Picture Punch sheet and stick it against the blue border in the bottom right-hand corner on the card. Cut the top left-hand corner off. Cut the rectangle with the Father Christmas out of the Allura embossing vellum, emboss it and use double-sided adhesive tape to stick it behind the yellow frame. Use glitter glue in different colours to draw around the Father Christmas on the red card and allow it to dry. Punch Father Christmases and use 3D glue to stick them along the diagonal line of the yellow card. Stick a Christmas wish on the card.

*I wish to thank Vaessen Creative for making all the materials used in this book available.*

1.

2.

3.